songs we used to dance to

Copyright © 2021 by courtney marie

All rights reserved. No portion of this book may be reproduced or transmitted by any means whatsoever without the express written permission of the publisher.

Printed in the United States of America

First Edition, 2022

ISBN 978-0-9985554-8-5
GMGB04

Cover design by Darin Bradley
Cover art by Cameron Cox
Interior layout and design by Aaron Leis

Poems in this collection have appeared in or are forthcoming from *beestung literary journal*, *The Boiler*, *Crow & Cross Keys*, and *warning lines magazine*.

Goliad Media is a production house based in Denton, TX, showcasing art, literature, music, and mixed media. We dream of empty places.

goliadmedia.net

songs we used to dance to

courtney marie

GOODIVA

to everyone fighting for a better world

contents

no good very bad	9
things were never like you think they used to be	11
i am not myself	12
we're all doing our best	13
which is never enough	14
death of the party	15
a proper revolt	16
talking to strangers	17
happy birthday to my ghost	19
~~*things that didn't matter*~~	20
things that didn't matter	22
this country is a hungry fist	24
a raindrop reflects on the burning plain	25
everything is fine	27
artist statement	29
somewhere in the world it was midnight, bastille day	30
phased	32
a love story	33
where was i	35
what to expect when you are expecting nothing	37
i forgot the safe word again	39
my ghost attempts to live again	41
my ghost finds everything tedious	42
this is how you get ants	43
maybe there will be dancing	45
overwhelmed	47
our love is a rainforest on fire	49
seven year itch	50
it's better to just stay home	52

full moon blues	*53*
divorce city	*54*
sorry i'm late	*55*
unsettled / settling	*56*
i have already memorized the poems i am not yet brave enough to write	*57*
you cannot erase nightmares by calling them dreams	*59*
anything for you	*61*
help me / i'm disappearing	*62*
could be worse	*65*
it's always something	*67*
in which i ask you to help reenact a dream i had	*68*
a forest of contradictions	*70*
from what i understand this is totally normal end of the world sex	*71*
abandoned community garden	*73*
summer is coming	*75*
if the world is ending	*76*
always never	*78*
it is okay to always be becoming	*80*
how to save the world	*81*
it starts like this	*83*
what is reality	*85*
there are many ways to be invisible	*87*
somewhere out there it's all on fire	*89*
my ghost has noticed something is wrong	*91*
things are probably best this way	*92*
nothing is what it seems	*93*
my grief does not know how to sleep	*94*
so much can happen in a year	*96*
missing: ghost	*98*
can you hear me now	*99*
we say goodbye to things	*100*
what now	*103*
a better world was possible	*105*

how we survived a pandemic	*106*
maybe my ghost is gone forever	*108*
special occasions	*109*
what we missed most	*110*
nothing will ever be the same	*111*
self portrait as panic attack	*112*
self portrait as first poem on new medication	*113*
nothing had changed and everything was different	*114*
we did things we knew would kill us	*115*
missing: poet	*116*
laying awake at night thinking about other people's lives	*117*
the end	*121*

NO GOOD VERY BAD NO GOOD VERY BAD NO GOOD VERY BAD
NO GOOD VERY BAD NO GOOD VERY BAD NO GOOD VERY BAD
NO GOOD VERY BAD NO GOOD VERY BAD NO GOOD VERY BAD
NO GOOD VERY BAD NO GOOD VERY BAD NO GOOD VERY BAD
NO GOOD VERY BAD NO GOOD VERY BAD NO GOOD VERY BAD
NO GOOD VERY BAD NO GOOD VERY BAD NO GOOD VERY BAD
NO GOOD VERY BAD NO GOOD VERY BAD NO GOOD VERY BAD
NO GOOD VERY BAD NO GOOD VERY BAD NO GOOD VERY BAD
NO GOOD VERY BAD NO GOOD VERY BAD NO GOOD VERY BAD
NO GOOD VERY BAD NO GOOD VERY BAD NO GOOD VERY BAD
NO GOOD VERY BAD NO GOOD VERY BAD NO GOOD VERY BAD
NO GOOD VERY BAD NO GOOD VERY BAD NO GOOD VERY BAD
NO GOOD VERY BAD NO GOOD VERY BAD NO GOOD VERY BAD
NO GOOD VERY BAD NO GOOD VERY BAD NO GOOD VERY BAD
NO GOOD VERY BAD NO GOOD VERY BAD NO GOOD VERY BAD
NO GOOD VERY BAD NO GOOD VERY BAD NO GOOD VERY BAD
NO GOOD VERY BAD NO GOOD VERY BAD NO GOOD VERY BAD
NO GOOD VERY BAD NO GOOD VERY BAD NO GOOD VERY BAD
NO GOOD VERY BAD NO GOOD VERY BAD NO GOOD VERY BAD
NO GOOD VERY BAD NO GOOD VERY BAD NO GOOD VERY BAD
NO GOOD VERY BAD NO GOOD VERY BAD NO GOOD VERY BAD
NO GOOD VERY BAD NO GOOD VERY BAD NO GOOD VERY BAD
NO GOOD VERY BAD NO GOOD VERY BAD NO GOOD VERY BAD
NO GOOD VERY BAD NO GOOD VERY BAD NO GOOD VERY BAD
NO GOOD VERY BAD NO GOOD VERY BAD NO GOOD VERY BAD

```
things were never like you think they used to be
```

~~there was beauty before the ruin~~
~~though we didn't see it~~

all the wars kept us busy

we were armed with answers
        in the shape of twitter threads
we solved problems
        with money
        which was a problem

we were obsessed with plastic things
wrapped in plastic
wrapped in plastic
wrapped in plastic
wrapped in plastic
all of which we threw away

we liked things to be so easy

we were so afraid to love anything

```
i am not myself
```

i stopped listening to music unless you count long cicada screams. i stopped writing poems in my head. forgot entire words for days. got lost in the unmarked map of my mind. sometimes i cannot see what others see, which is a [blessing / curse]. i stopped writing letters promising [i'll be home soon / that i'll write again soon]. i still haven't climbed down from the tree in my grandparent's yard. still haven't said [goodbye / i forgive you]. still don't know why i couldn't speak up. still haven't told you what happened to me.

forgive me, for i don't want to be here.

i am a shadow of someone who was never there.

forgive me, for i am not myself

& so much of life has been trying to survive it.

forgive me, a reluctant ghost.

we're all doing our best

my ghost volunteers on holidays
(blankets & soup)
  gives all she can
  tries to sing
  wants to be happy

but sometimes when she is home alone she wails
& frightens the neighborhood

i apologize via email

  i'm sorry for all the screaming

she isn't always like this, i write

she just wants so desperately
  to be anything but a ghost

`which is never enough`

they add up
        the things we can't make peace with

alive so close to the end game

for some of us
once the sadness enters
it never goes away

how do you keep moving
        knowing everything will burn?

the good news is i'm writing poetry again
the bad news is it won't save the world

only one thing to do:
        throw a party

death of the party

i ghost on every party before i get there
a bundle of frayed nerves beneath my skin
i've picked up worrying
i worry all the time
broken thoughts on a loop

~~*i stay busy so my mind doesn't have time to kill me*~~

these days i identify as something in-between
i identify as anxiety attack
a high-functioning breakdown
a cat on its last life
something i can't yet articulate
but my chest is full of doom

the death of the party
can barely leave the house
can barely watch the news

i am sick like the world is sick
i miss people who have forgotten me
myself most of all

sometimes i'm afraid maybe i'm the ghost
& everybody
[knows /
is afraid to tell me]

`a proper revolt`

my ghost has a crush on the moon
[there's so much to do]

> our whole lives spent preparing for a proper revolt

there is talk of rising up
i am ready for it

> a better world is possible & i want to see it happen

my ghost has nothing left to lose
for weeks has been asking for a quiet night alone

> has been bringing home tulips & stone fruit

has been sighing
i don't have time for this

> but my ghost insists

we go outside
[there's so much to do]

> every day another protest

my ghost is daydreaming & i am shouting
WHAT IF WE ACTUALLY ATE THE RICH?

> yes the time for the revolution is now

my ghost is grinning like a fool
IMAGINE WHAT WE COULD DO IF WE WORKED TOGETHER

    what if we were a hive of bees?

    what if we communicated by dancing?

the moon looms overheard
we don't say anything but i can hear my ghost softly crying

        elsewhere
            everything collapsing

things are so bad i can't keep up
we're ripe for a riot, but everyone's at work

    (i see what's happening here)

we build a fire under the next full moon and make plans to build a guillotine
we ask what we are ready to give up

    everything is changing

`talking to strangers`

late one night as the bar is closing
someone i was talking to asks my name
& though
>*[we have very little in common /*
>*i never want to see them again /*
>*i hate my name]*
i tell them anyway

then i lean close and whisper
I DON'T KNOW WHO I AM

it's true (what they say)

i barely live here

i barely live anywhere

```
happy birthday to my ghost
```

every year she insists we throw a party even bigger than the last. it's like she doesn't even know she's dead. we invite everyone we know and hope they'll get along. soon the house is full of [artists / poets / bakers / musicians / ghouls / witches / ghosts]. it's seventy-three degrees in january because the planet is dying. my ghost insists we all take psychedelics. it's her birthday, after all. suddenly the whole place is glittering. everyone shares a pack of cigarettes because we all quit smoking. maybe it's the drugs, but i feel okay. i tell someone this is my favorite dream. we blow dandelion seeds. there are wishes in our hair. i haven't read the news in three days. i try not to think about it. try to enjoy the moment. try to soak up being alive, even though it can be terrible. i cry because i don't want any of it to end. it takes five people to light all the birthday candles. no one sings happy birthday because it's a horrible song. instead, the radio sings, and we laugh. my ghost wants to kiss everyone on the mouth. we had our cake but forgot to eat it.

and every now and then
i escape to the silence outside it all
to savor the already fleeting memory
to listen to the rumble of voices rising
from a house full of people i love
alive and living well

~~things that didn't matter~~

there were many flowers but no shade

all my poems had depressing titles like
DON'T GET YOUR HOPES UP

i was always outdoing myself with existential grief

we all developed anxiety disorders

& everything felt worse in summer
before the winter dread set in

sometimes we built a fire in the yard of the house
on the land that was stolen and stolen and stolen
and sold to me, which i thought about all the time
not knowing what to do about it

we had a thousand impossible dreams
crushed daily by the systems that claimed to save us

we were in love
regardless of how badly we knew it was all going to end

the broken house we were born in
was built on recklessness and greed
& in our inherited selfishness
oblivious to our own demise:

we still made music

we still grew flowers
& watched the birds in the evening

we still made love sometimes
& laughed when we felt happy

& sometimes we really were happy
among the flowers

sometimes we truly believed
we would be saved

```
things that didn't matter
```

                    sometimes we made magic

sometimes we believed in ourselves

though so much was considered
      [predestined /
      coincidence /
      pull of gravity toward earth]

sometimes it was worth not giving up

it felt like
      [mother's tears
           [frequent /
           lonely] /
      the first time we saw fire /
      the last goodbye]

sometimes our memories failed us

    so much for childhood

        we [moved often /
        grew up fast]

we missed things we never had
(there were so many things to have)

we were grateful for so little
we had the audacity to

    [ignore sunsets /
    kill senselessly]

our ripples became tsunamis &
    [many of us died /
    we were never happy]

some of us had everything & some of us had nothing
~~*& by the time we woke up*~~
    ~~*nothing could be done*~~

we kept going

    discovered fire and burned the house down

```
this country is a hungry fist
```

best known for being the meanest kid on the playground
a murderous villain who grew up angry and entitled

this country
is not like other countries
it speaks no language
shows no mercy
feasts on the dreams of the innocent
filthy with cash
bloody with debt & disgrace

this country is a hungry fist
seven deadly sins personified
too lazy to repent
too proud to give up
its bloodthirsty temper
the hedonism that consumes
everything in its path

this country is a manufacturer
of sorrows
the opposite of hope
and we break
under the weight
of its vicious
mistakes

[& we
        (the people)
                are afraid of what happens next]

`a raindrop reflects on a burning plain`

so when they set the family's fields on fire
do you imagine we will run or stay?
have they forgotten we have [everything / nothing] to lose?
do they not remember how we stood our ground before?
    [where our seeds were born /
    where every fruit was gently named]?

& when the blaze meets the shingles of our homes
there will be no time to waste
we will leave the pebbles gathered on the window panes
& in a heartbeat
    take stock of all that will be lost

with only ourselves left to save
we will fall heavy and all at once
sacrificing the first and last of
everything we'd become

& though i am very small
    merely a teardrop

i will remember that together we become river
together we can be ocean or storm
    calm or furious
    warm or cold
    danger or safety

i will remember we are cleansing:
    glasses full & hearts breaking

i will remember the power the people hold
    & the way a canyon floods in a flash

& while the sound of one raindrop is never heard
    the strength of many can drown
        even the most vicious fire burning on the plains

EVERYTHING IS FINE EVERYTHING IS FINE EVERYTHING IS FINE
EVERYTHING IS FINE EVERYTHING IS FINE EVERYTHING IS FINE
EVERYTHING IS FINE EVERYTHING IS FINE EVERYTHING IS FINE
EVERYTHING IS FINE EVERYTHING IS FINE EVERYTHING IS FINE
EVERYTHING IS FINE EVERYTHING IS FINE EVERYTHING IS FINE
EVERYTHING IS FINE EVERYTHING IS FINE EVERYTHING IS FINE
EVERYTHING IS FINE EVERYTHING IS FINE EVERYTHING IS FINE
EVERYTHING IS FINE EVERYTHING IS FINE EVERYTHING IS FINE
EVERYTHING IS FINE EVERYTHING IS FINE EVERYTHING IS FINE
EVERYTHING IS FINE EVERYTHING IS FINE EVERYTHING IS FINE
EVERYTHING IS FINE EVERYTHING IS FINE EVERYTHING IS FINE
EVERYTHING IS FINE EVERYTHING IS FINE EVERYTHING IS FINE
EVERYTHING IS FINE EVERYTHING IS FINE EVERYTHING IS FINE
EVERYTHING IS FINE EVERYTHING IS FINE EVERYTHING IS FINE
EVERYTHING IS FINE EVERYTHING IS FINE EVERYTHING IS FINE
EVERYTHING IS FINE EVERYTHING IS FINE EVERYTHING IS FINE
EVERYTHING IS FINE EVERYTHING IS FINE EVERYTHING IS FINE
EVERYTHING IS FINE EVERYTHING IS FINE EVERYTHING IS FINE
EVERYTHING IS FINE EVERYTHING IS FINE EVERYTHING IS FINE
EVERYTHING IS FINE EVERYTHING IS FINE EVERYTHING IS FINE
EVERYTHING IS FINE EVERYTHING IS FINE EVERYTHING IS FINE
EVERYTHING IS FINE EVERYTHING IS FINE EVERYTHING IS FINE
EVERYTHING IS FINE EVERYTHING IS FINE EVERYTHING IS FINE
EVERYTHING IS FINE EVERYTHING IS FINE EVERYTHING IS FINE
EVERYTHING IS FINE EVERYTHING IS FINE EVERYTHING IS FINE
EVERYTHING IS FINE EVERYTHING IS FINE EVERYTHING IS FINE
EVERYTHING IS FINE EVERYTHING IS FINE EVERYTHING IS FINE
EVERYTHING IS FINE EVERYTHING IS FINE EVERYTHING IS FINE

`artist statement`

we
      haunt
            this
                  place
                        now

```
somewhere in the world it was midnight, bastille day
```

    unrelated:
a coup where many people were killed

& the world is so frightening
i forget my own problems
    [dizzy /
    tired /
    hungry /
    weak]

when i look up from the news, something is wrong

i google {the symptoms for the twenty-eighth time}
i am rolling a joint
even though the website says
NO DRUGS OR ALCOHOL

on a sheet of paper i write down things i know i will forget
    [out of state /
    wednesday /
    cash only /
    taxi /
    eleven a.m.]
on the screen, they are telling civilians to avoid areas of conflict
    reports of gunfire

i am going to be sick

i google {what now?}

a man on the news says
THE FOOTAGE YOU ARE ABOUT TO SEE MAY BE DISTURBING
so many people are dead or dying

i google {what to wear to the clinic}
when people ask what's wrong
we agree that it is nothing
it is easiest to pretend that nothing is wrong
           at all times

but now i have the answer:
           [loose fitting clothes /
           turn off all electronics /
           empty your stomach]
what no one mentions
is how to conceal this growing sorrow

on tv, people are being told to take to the streets
a friend texts WHAT ARE YOU DOING TOMORROW?
and i nearly scream
           [right there at the bar /
           in the middle of happy hour]

& i feel numb like i have been crying for days except that i can't cry
until i do & then i can't stop & i still have so many questions like how
can i still be so scared of doctors when we are watching the world burn?

why would i bring another body into this horror?
how could i care for a child, even if i wanted one?

another friend writes a letter asking WHAT ARE YOU?

i reply:

i am beginning

i am my own end

```
phased
```

when you are a moon
sometimes you feel whole
& sometimes you are a sliver
& sometimes what looks like disappearing
is a natural reaction to constant motion

today the moon reminds me
*   we can always come back*

no matter what you are experiencing
*   you are beautiful*

& even the moon needs to take a break sometimes

a love story

> [finally /
> sometimes]

i admit that everything must change

when i feel low

i dress up real nice

& start walking

i pace the city

there are still so many places i haven't been

the beautiful thing about a street

is that it never ends

there is always somewhere to go

& when its really bad

i say shit out loud like

IT'S GOING TO BE OKAY

&

YOU ARE AN UNBREAKABLE BADASS

i try to say nice things to myself

i think about cutting my hair

`where was i`

*somewhere leaning hard against the invisible sensations
in a nearly condemned house turned gallery showcasing
        all the strangeness our early twenties had to offer
chaotic photos & facepaint & resin-filled cups
flickering video tapes & grotesque sculptures looming
& a boyfriend about to break his arm
flirting with someone else*

*which was okay because
i was on some next level shit
feeling the tension of the room
courting the night with nothing
but a ghostly wingman
& my drunken inhibitions*

*we tried my hottest lines
HAVE YOU BEEN HERE BEFORE?
ARE YOU AS SAD AS ME?*

*i discovered a room full of sand
        & beach chairs
        & thought about how
we're always conceptualizing relaxation
we're always trying to make the best of a short stick
or a free keg
or a boyfriend with a broken arm*

*we grinned & beared it that night
        my ghost & i
i know now it will get better & worse
i painted my face blue & stripped to my underwear*

*i've always wanted to belong somewhere
there was no reason to cry yet
        but i wanted to
the hot tub was cold
the stars were brighter than i remembered*

*later, my wet body in the dirt
        i realized
        something in me is broken too
when i return
        everyone is falling asleep or making out
& i frighten myself in the mirror*

*i am too young to know everything has gone wrong
too ignorant to know how to fix anything broken*

*YOU'RE NOBODY TO ME
        i told myself*

what to expect when you are expecting nothing

there will be chairs
so many empty chairs
& whole rooms sparse and sprawling

there will be a glass of vodka swaying as if held by an invisible hand
                    [hypnotized /
                    dancing /
                    transparent]

a shadow speaking its own language
begging to go home

there will be the car running
and your exoskeleton in the driver's seat
refusing to leave
refusing to let anyone inside

                    ~~sometimes this is how you keep the peace~~

you keep humming the tune of a song you don't know the name of
        one we used to dance to

keep waking up (there aren't many options)
keep deadlines (no one must know)
keep commitments
keep standing upright
keep smiling
keep it in

a record skipping over and over and no one in the room to stop it
(maybe soon the needle will grow tired and silence itself)

until then
keep up the performance
keep the glass balanced delicately between two fingers
while twirling and laughing at something no one else can see

keep telling yourself
    [to breathe /
    that no bad dream will last forever]

keep billowing
    [a curl of smoke trapped in a bell jar /
    a flameless moth at twilight]

keep telling yourself there will be a tomorrow
(the worst that can happen is you will be wrong)

keep wondering how long you will get away with this soft existence
keep counting the minutes down to nothing
keep telling everyone you're okay
    everything is fine

i forgot the safe word again

      [it's not you /
      it's me]

not
      [so much self sabotage /
      so much as an absence of self]

to disappear is to not be hurt (again)

~~*there are no accidents*~~

how strange to be
      [frozen /
      in the heat of the moment]

AND TERRIFIED, *i say*
      [too many times /
      wanting to leave /
      wanting to stay]

heart too
      [broken /
      sick /
      tired /
      queer /
      angry]

to fully communicate how afraid i am to
      [love /
      be loved]

but longing to tell you ~~*everything*~~

the way i love
        a mess:

                [unidentified /
                reclassified /
                unhinged]

sometimes my weakness is all i have to give

i worry
        [about my memory /
        that i am too much /
        until i am buried under the weight of all i meant to say]

this is dedicated to
        [all the poems i will not write /
        you]

the (mis)adventures of a danger queen
a candle we couldn't help but burn
an ode to
        [melted flesh /
        a kind of death /
        what was soon to be lost]

i worry
        [it will never be enough /
        that i am losing the words to describe something holy /
        that forgetting is easy]

& we're running out of time

`my ghost attempts to live again`

my ghost is preoccupied with death

    she didn't mean for you to find out this way

we have attempted to exorcise this compulsion for many years

    but one cannot eat one's own heart

```
my ghost finds everything tedious
```

she is buzzing
pacing / fidgety
anxiously waiting
for something to happen

i am counting down the days to nothing
all around us
the noise of a planet dying
of war versus war

the future dwindles but we are in love
we are buying postcard stamps and lingerie

we can agree on one thing:
if the world is ending
we will go down burning

only i want a revolution

& my ghost wants group sex by candlelight

`this is how you get ants`

(first: lose your mind)

tell them they are welcome to come over any time

write them long letters about
the contents of your kitchen cabinets

keep expired food
buy fresh fruit

dust the rims of drained wine glasses with sugar

get to know their mothers
send them chocolates on their birthday

cook but forget to eat
take a lot of walks

leave all the windows open
& pour apple juice on the sills

call them and ask them what they think
about your new poem

tell them to be honest
tell them it might rain

build a house right on top of a massive colony
somewhere in the desert
& let the faucets drip

*go on vacation
leave out candy wrappers*

*consider buying a carton of poison
just in case things get out of hand*

*meanwhile give them nicknames
and joke around*

*ants actually have a very good
sense of humor*

`maybe there will be dancing`

maybe it will be on the steps of a museum
or in the rush of a passing train

                      maybe the sky will be heavy with clouds

maybe you will recognize me in a crowd
& offer your hands outstretched

                      maybe mine will be shaking
                      both of us present in this spell

maybe this will be a page torn out of a storybook
dislocated but rewriting itself
        with patience and purpose

                      one of us will speak first

maybe it will be you or maybe it will be me

                      & maybe it won't matter
                      that we can't help ourselves but wave

maybe we were built for the undercurrent

                      maybe i am stronger than i feel

maybe there is a place that isn't a place
that we will find there

maybe there will be a parade
maybe there will be dancing
maybe there will be silence

maybe we will get lost

and find our way back again

*OVERWHELMED OVERWHELMED OVERWHELMED OVERWHELMED
OVERWHELMED OVERWHELMED OVERWHELMED OVERWHELMED
OVERWHELMED OVERWHELMED OVERWHELMED OVERWHELMED
OVERWHELMED OVERWHELMED OVERWHELMED OVERWHELMED
OVERWHELMED OVERWHELMED OVERWHELMED OVERWHELMED
OVERWHELMED OVERWHELMED OVERWHELMED OVERWHELMED
OVERWHELMED OVERWHELMED OVERWHELMED OVERWHELMED
OVERWHELMED OVERWHELMED OVERWHELMED OVERWHELMED
OVERWHELMED OVERWHELMED OVERWHELMED OVERWHELMED
OVERWHELMED OVERWHELMED OVERWHELMED OVERWHELMED
OVERWHELMED OVERWHELMED OVERWHELMED OVERWHELMED
OVERWHELMED OVERWHELMED OVERWHELMED OVERWHELMED
OVERWHELMED OVERWHELMED OVERWHELMED OVERWHELMED
OVERWHELMED OVERWHELMED OVERWHELMED OVERWHELMED
OVERWHELMED OVERWHELMED OVERWHELMED OVERWHELMED
OVERWHELMED OVERWHELMED OVERWHELMED OVERWHELMED
OVERWHELMED OVERWHELMED OVERWHELMED OVERWHELMED
OVERWHELMED OVERWHELMED OVERWHELMED OVERWHELMED
OVERWHELMED OVERWHELMED OVERWHELMED OVERWHELMED
OVERWHELMED OVERWHELMED OVERWHELMED OVERWHELMED
OVERWHELMED OVERWHELMED OVERWHELMED OVERWHELMED
OVERWHELMED OVERWHELMED OVERWHELMED OVERWHELMED
OVERWHELMED OVERWHELMED OVERWHELMED OVERWHELMED*

`our love is a rainforest on fire`

there is nothing more tragic than our most precious resource smoldering

as if we could live like this forever

        as if resources were infinite

                as if there were no limits

as if, without the proper care

this could be anything but devastating

`seven year itch`

i want to talk about how we shed layers of skin
for years until we are no longer ourselves

i am interested in this rebirth

i am afraid of the space i take up
whether invisible or on display
      a mockery or ghost
sometimes too much
often not enough

i picture a snail
slow moving and simple:
      are they also always thinking of things
      that are safe versus things that are not safe?

i started a list of things i want people to know
without ever having to tell them:
      the new common language
      & i will read it to you if i ever have the courage to spare

the truth is i am on a side quest
to learn every definition of loss
so i can remind you we're not yet gone
      that there are things in this world older than fear
      & that to be soft is (sometimes) to be unbreakable

my secret is to pretend for a moment
      that i am in love with everyone i meet

                                                ~~*i am in love with you*~~

*& wonder in which ways
we will ask each other to change*

it's better to just stay home

an old woman at the grocery store
pulls my hair near the carrots
she says STOP BOTHERING MY SON
i hand her some cabbage
& buy some milk

the walk home is slow
& i am heavy with the memory of a child
how they smile so sweetly
until they're old enough to know better

they said i would be born a boy
with the stolen name of a holy man
      instead i am something else
         confused by what everyone has had to say about it

full moon blues

i have [been finding comfort in things that make me feel small / considered disappearing]. i am reassured by the stars and their stories. i look up to the moon. i find solace in her glow. i slow dance with my ghost. we are all we have left.

```
divorce city
```

ten years later
    i visit the bookshop
        where i once worked

they remember me
    but not my name
        which is not the same

the diner is still there
    but the cafe is gone

the italian restaurant
    was replaced with cheap sandwiches

pawn shop still intact

library the same as ever

the house on palm street
    has seen better days
    and honestly
    so have i

sorry i'm late

[i got stuck in an existential shame spiral /
i forgot how to leave the house /
there's a global pandemic /
nothing matters anymore /
the cat needed attention /
i was busy screaming /
i forgot what day it is /
i forgot how to drive /
i was getting drunk /
time is a construct /
i'm not sure i exist /
i didn't want to go /
i forgot who i am /
i'm tired of trying /
the void called /
i was crying /

nothing is real]

```
unsettling / settled
```

heat source. invisible danger. an intense fear of fright. a comforting hand. but can't shake the horror. wild imaginations. shattered mirrors. a character in a book. they try to write. soft sounds. torches light needles pricking nighttime. a sideways glance at the clock. a lesser villain. a greater comfort. an experiment lost in the treetops. a stray bone in the field. a massive hill of fire ants. two men drive by in a car. someone is waving. they don't know anyone. they hide their face. they climb too high. there is no way down. they bruise their knee. scratch their elbow. write a postcard. to someone they don't know. turn their life into a poem. make it interesting. read a book they wish they wrote. cough up a hundred excuses. learn how to type again.

look at the stars. no. really. look. here. there is nothing to be afraid of. the doors are unbolted. they peer behind shower curtains. there is nothing there. they sing together. large raindrops falling. make love in the shower. oil and water. the beat of summer storms. change places. share a drawing. birds. circle of life. experience death. come out alright. (do you want to talk about it?) photographs. a happy place. re-learn to read. finish a book. ignore the reflection. ignore the sad things. have another glass of wine.

```
i have already memorized the poems i
am not yet brave enough to write
```

they are a crowded orphanage
a house full of hungry children i cannot feed

they are the silence of an unmarked grave

i know their shape by heart / jagged concrete
sharp as needle point / invisible to the naked eye
a shard of glass singing the inside of a fingernail

i am ashamed they remain unwritten / that i have become an echo of
    silence
these all consuming terrors / a shroud laid to rest over peaceful dreams

quietly i gather the pieces
i count them / i name them
    a darkness of youth
    a tragedy of innocence
    a disappointment of trust

they fill a thick / imaginary book detailing fractures and betrayals
everything remembered too often and too well

i have already memorized the poems i am not yet brave enough to write
(and i tell you this because i may never be)

there's whole pages of damnation / of demons exposed
    a revenge of bones
    a list of names i won't let near my tongue
    a sorrow of family
    a silhouette of a house on the verge of collapse
    an exhaustion of memory

bones buried in places far removed
spells written as a last resort

a reckoning of fear

`you cannot erase nightmares by calling them dreams`

up close it was ugly
the landscape a landfill
& how eagerly you (the antagonist) climbed heaps of filth
    [to reach the top /
    to leave me behind]

& how careless to pretend
    the screaming had subsided
    when all you did was ascend

only thinking of getting high
    crushing me under avalanche
    & oh my god it was bad but got worse

every day wasted
    in willful negligence
your efforts to silence
        the truth
    [so /
    & /
    instead]

it happened again & again & again & again & again & again & again
  & again

        eroding everything

& how quick you moved on
    or learned to play the savior stabbing

& how effortlessly you stole sanity
    became a barricade to the only escape
        (crumbling)

& how hard you worked to save yourself
    while i lay buried
lost in nightmares you claimed were dreams
    (you claimed were beautiful)

& i wonder if you have ever dreamt of being
    something holy
    to hold & cherish
    only to become
    an apple consumed
    to the core

    only to become
    [trash /
    disposable /
    submerged]

discarded by someone
    trying to be
        what you
            should have been

`anything for you`

i start a letter that is more condemnation than forgiveness. time has ceased to exist and i am frozen in horror. noticing what i could not. would not. it is all too familiar. and i know what comes next.

you don't need to worry because i blame myself. i would hate for you to hate me because i hate you. i would rather choke on it. become a shadow of myself. a copy of a copy of myself. i know. i'll ignore it. i'll ignore the clawing in my gut. if it never happened. if i believe hard enough it never happened. but then. why does it keep happening. why do i say yes when i mean no. or did i say no. or did i not. (if i did you wouldn't right?) if i told you something was wrong it wouldn't. keep happening. or what if i ran from the room screaming. you wouldn't. would you? what if i made it all up. what if i didn't say anything. at all. since nothing said can't be real. nothing can't hurt me. what if i said stop. what if i said not tonight. not ever again. what if i ended it. would you stop then. would you. stop.

```
help me / i'm disappearing
```

"i'm sorry it's been so long and

      [i'm sorry to be starting with an apology /
      it's probably best i leave this in a message]

i'm not sure where to start
      i keep meaning to call you to tell you

      [i miss you and think of you so often /
      i keep wanting to write you a letter]

but the truth is i am afraid

      [i have run out of pleasant things to talk about /
      i am running out of time /
      the last letter i tried to write you said, ~~help me~~ /
      ~~i'm disappearing~~]

which felt like too much of a bummer
      so i didn't send it
i haven't been
      [sleeping well /
      eating well /
      breathing well]

          [i'm on edge /
          i'm not myself]

i tell you this because even at my worst

      [i love you]

and i want you to know

    [i love you]

        [even if i don't know how best to show it /
        even if i'm not sure how to love myself /
        even if sometimes i'm not sure about tomorrow /
        even if i don't have the right thing to say or you
            don't have the right thing to say /
        even if we can't say anything at all]

i tell you this

    [because we're all we have /
    because
        despite it all
            maybe i don't want to disappear]"

COULD BE WORSE COULD BE WORSE COULD BE WORSE COULD
BE WORSE COULD BE WORSE COULD BE WORSE COULD BE
WORSE COULD BE WORSE COULD BE WORSE COULD BE WORSE
COULD BE WORSE COULD BE WORSE COULD BE WORSE COULD
BE WORSE COULD BE WORSE COULD BE WORSE COULD BE
WORSE COULD BE WORSE COULD BE WORSE COULD BE WORSE
COULD BE WORSE COULD BE WORSE COULD BE WORSE COULD
BE WORSE COULD BE WORSE COULD BE WORSE COULD BE
WORSE COULD BE WORSE COULD BE WORSE COULD BE WORSE
COULD BE WORSE COULD BE WORSE COULD BE WORSE COULD
BE WORSE COULD BE WORSE COULD BE WORSE COULD BE
WORSE COULD BE WORSE COULD BE WORSE COULD BE WORSE
COULD BE WORSE COULD BE WORSE COULD BE WORSE COULD
BE WORSE COULD BE WORSE COULD BE WORSE COULD BE
WORSE COULD BE WORSE COULD BE WORSE COULD BE WORSE
COULD BE WORSE COULD BE WORSE COULD BE WORSE COULD
BE WORSE COULD BE WORSE COULD BE WORSE COULD BE
WORSE COULD BE WORSE COULD BE WORSE COULD BE WORSE
COULD BE WORSE COULD BE WORSE COULD BE WORSE COULD
BE WORSE COULD BE WORSE COULD BE WORSE COULD BE
WORSE COULD BE WORSE COULD BE WORSE COULD BE WORSE

```
it's always something
```

earthquakes in puerto rico
& in texas, a hurricane approaches

> *~~i know this is a bad time to bring it up but~~*
> *~~i didn't want to be again today~~*

everything on fire
burning
the west coast
& australia

> *r's letters from california sound worried*
>
> *h's dog died this morning*
>
> *some friends came over and we cried*
> *& played a game of farkle*
> *not knowing what else to do*

unrest everywhere

> *~~my head is full of screaming~~*
>
> *usually we act like everything is fine*
>
> *but we're all so sad*
>
> *& i still can't write poems*
>
> *that will make anything better*

```
in which i ask you to help reenact a dream i had
```

not the one where the walls became quicksand
      eating the rooms of the house where we lived
not the one where we hid in an abandoned schoolhouse
          always running
not the one where i kiss your girlfriend
      or the one that returns each full moon
          where we hide in a cave
              listening to the echoes of lost conversations

not the one where i am a bird
      & you are a cat trying to make up its mind
not the one where we speak in another language
      (one that has not yet been documented)
or the one where we must construct a sling for my broken arm
      in order to travel back to the place
          where we first said yes yes yes yes yes

not the dream about the window
      (not any of the window-dreams)
not the people-watching
the close-up raindrops
the clumsy love
or the one where your voice begins to read to me
    [disembodied /
    impossible]
        because you are dead

& it wasn't the one where you stand in my kitchen
      drinking milk & later
          we are rats sharing a prison cell
it wasn't the one where we are starlings on the same wire

overlooking a beach
where you warn me the water is cold
& beg me not to leave

it's not the half-dream where i write you letters
& burn them as i go
or where you tell me your new name
& our chance meeting becomes a clerical error
or the one where we never actually meet at all

in its accurate re-creation we speak frankly of the price:
IT COSTS TOO MUCH FOR TOO LITTLE
& we're broke

& i want to tell you [that not everything is a dream /
that some things cannot be taken back]

but instead (like the dream) i insist i understand

this is normal

lying on two separate beds in a strange room
reaching but not quite
your eyes shining like sunshine on piano keys

while i explain why i can't go outside
explain that love is like
a room full of windows
each one with a different
[view /
constellation /
light]

a forest of contradictions

it helps to know where you're going but not really / a sturdy moral compass won't save us / this is [the twenty first century / two roads diverged] / & i think [i would prefer to fly / i'm tired of thinking] / ready to jump / or burrow depending on the season / is it just me or is it cold in here / good thing we have so many layers / yes no yes no yes no maybe / good thing we have grown so used to disappointment / ~~not dead yet~~ */ grown stronger than the trees / for all the things that have tried to kill us / we still exist / welcome to the minefield / watch your [step / tongue] / i try to think before i speak / but not too hard / sometimes it's so [good / bad] i think maybe [i could live here / i'm going to die]*

```
from what i understand this is
totally normal end of the world sex
```

we are panting
the world is spinning out of reach
we can't be held responsible

please will someone hold me
tell me it can be forever
or that nothing is forever
or crush me like dust in your hands

tell me i am beautiful
have we ever been happier?
the timing is
    [perfect /
    tragic]:

we left the party
    [to go home together /
    & it all came crashing down]

why am i so turned on?

                                 ~~*no one writes me letters anymore*~~

we weave through painted streets
howling

we get lost but
    i didn't want to be at a sad party anyway

at least we have each other
though we took too many drugs
to remember it in the morning

but we'll do it again
and again
and again

until the fire finally reaches our house
until we're swept away by flood
until we're carried away screaming
until the war eats itself whole
until the wells dry up
until the drought is never ending

how romantic:
perhaps this is how things were
    [always /
     meant to be]

`abandoned community garden`

*(if you're looking for somewhere to momentarily escape
from the shambling wreckage of late-stage capitalism)*

*we know just the place
where remnants of what was once shared freely
are anything but desolate*

*here thrive
    [forgotten perennials /
    enthusiastic mint /
    overgrown oregano /
    sprawling thyme] creeping past
the bricks & decaying logs
that once kept them contained*

*rusted tomato cages
unnecessary for the withered stems
    of seasons passed*

*it's peaceful here
    in this neglected place
where my ghost and i
    depart from an afternoon stroll
    to languish a while
touching the leaves gently
    fingertips smelling of peppermint & lavender*

*steeping in a world given up on
    but refusing to let go*

i relate to whoever first
    [tilled the soil /
    built the boxes]
& repurposed the window frames
        to protect the seeds as they sprouted

how they must have told their friends
    THIS IS WHERE WE'LL GROW

i hunger for the feasts they imagined
imagine [how they cared for the mother plants /
    tended to seedlings /
    them out here with their [gentle dreams /
        freshly turned compost /
        dirty hands]]

isn't it so exciting to start something new?
to be together, aching for something wholesome?
isn't it charming:
    how we want to feel like we're helping?

my ghost is frolicking among the wild onions
    & i've found
(hidden below the flowering herbs)
    [a strawberry patch /
    berries bursting /
    a happy anthill /
    no one who needs what anyone's selling]

just a tiny patch of nature
reclaiming her time
    becoming herself again

`summer is coming`

but the sunlight will be a different sort of bright
    where nothing grows

a vast desert of what we could have done differently

there will be no television special
    there's nothing special about how our way of living
    has brought on the extinction of everything

besides
    the ratings would be terrible

the way this ends
    will be more disappointing than every bad tv show

there will be no steadfast castles
no magic swords
no tiger kings
no blue eyed zombies of death
no wolves to save us

just [countless species fading /
    irreversible mistakes]

just endless summer
    stretching forever and ever

just everything that ever was
    moving on without us

```
if the world is ending
```

when the party's over
        we'll be feeling nostalgic

we'll leave the boat rocking
we'll climb down to the shore

              ~~*do you want to come back to my place*~~
              ~~*& read each other poems til dawn?*~~

i'll offer to drive us home
        so long as you don't mind listening to
        a playlist of songs we used to dance to

(i'll apologize when they make us cry
        in the whataburger drive thru)

              ~~*have we ever been so happy?*~~

my ghost asks how i fall in love so easily
but she's one to talk

              ~~*do you think this is it?*~~

i like how you scream in the car with me
& make promises you'll never keep

              ~~*do you think the world is ending?*~~

we go together like sad and alone
& i never minded an empty handed lover
        so long as they kept me dreaming

  & i'm learning to trust the stars
       who have always said i crave
       something unanchored and nihilistic

              ~~*do you think we could save each other?*~~

so if nothing else matters
i would fly across the country for you
would walk forty city blocks for you
would almost carry a child for you
would eat my own heart for you
would face my fears for you
would take the fall for you
would abandon ship
would drown

```
always never
```

i look up the definition of GASLIGHTING *one more time*
    to make sure i'm not losing my mind

    it's true
i have [always / never] been wrong
[always / never] understood

i choose my poison
nesting in a house of shadows

[always / never] [here / there]
                                       ~~*& terribly certain*~~

i want to be a different mirror
a whole person
not [target / opponent]
not ferry-to-future-island
not next-bad-memory
not lunatic
not new book to burn

i do not remember the spells i have not conjured
i do not recall
    [filling my pockets with heavy rocks /
    the lake being quite this cold]
i don't know how we got here
i am dizzy from shaking my head

                         ~~NO~~

i have been in this place before
      & it is still full of ghosts

i move slow
      heavy with doubt

still trying to find my way home

it is okay to always be becoming

not every day can be a party

when you are broken it takes time to regenerate

whether you picture yourself a sprout
or a gardener
or a terrace in full bloom

you deserve water & light

it is okay to always be becoming

today is not yesterday
and tomorrow will be different

remember
there is purpose in seeking purpose
in planting a seed & watching it grow

like blossoms after a hard winter
your joy will rise from the darkness
& multiply

if you give yourself a chance
you too will have a garden

and a thousand new reasons to throw a party

```
how to save the world
```

write down all the ways
        we are connected
        [to each other /
        to every living thing]

replace [religion with art /
        art with magic /
        magic with wonder]

unmoor yourself from the conventional idea
        [that we cannot be saved /
        that our actions are too small /
        that to dream is hopeless]

make an inventory
        of everything holy
create a blueprint
        for future generations

light a candle for those we've lost
sing a song around a campfire
dance with fierce abandon
conjure spells to cast out evil
let go of the pieces that no longer fit

protest protest protest

bury your heart in the woods
        and return ready for war

we must fight
> [against being disposable /
> against the greed of the powerful]

write a letter to yourself
tell yourself that it is possible
> for love to flourish

tell yourself we're going to give it
> everything we've got

it starts like this

we return to try again

the sunlight opening itself into beams
against the glass of the windows of the house
    [where we live /
        where we have finally made a home]

a home as warm as we are
as the light fills the rooms with
an urgency i have never known:

the day is here!
get up!
it is the future!
it is moving onward
with or without us!

~~may we self destruct~~
        ~~before everything is ruined~~

WHAT IS REALITY WHAT IS REALITY

```
there are many ways to be invisible
```

my ghost pretends to write a poem
pushes her fingers past the keys of the machine
past the stained wood of the table
until she falls and catches herself swirling
a mist closing in on something
she can almost feel
she tells herself things like

A TRUE ARTIST WOULD NEVER GIVE UP!

a poet's strength is in the ability
to experience acts of living to their fullest!

feeling is writing
so she warms herself in winter
she attempts
        [the human act of loving /
        the art of swimming upward /
        to improve her condition]

she strains toward the sky, an axis of air, a parting gift from memory

        (has it been so long?)

she feins leaning against a wall in exhaustion but

        [the room isn't there /
        she doesn't exist]

sometimes
        she takes comfort in being dead

she reminds herself
*   there are many ways to be invisible*

```
somewhere out there it's all on fire
```

       & i am always waiting

(on what?)
       something that may never happen
                                         every time

this despair is relentless

       my ghost [is working overtime /
       haunting my ability to function]

reality is fluid
       i cannot
              concentrate on anything

impossible to think straight

i feel
       guilty for squandering so much time

i lose
       endless days to sadness

but every night we party

       a vicious carousel

i am
       turning into myself so slowly
       ~~*impossible not to be afraid of everything*~~

somewhere out there, it's all on fire

& i am just one body
      not dead

           (not yet)

`my ghost has noticed something is wrong`

she tries to get help

tries to go to the doctor
    but can't make it through the door
      & cries for awhile in the parking lot instead

(we always feel a little better after a good cry)

she texts an ex
    something sentimental

        she doesn't know what she wants

          she loses her phone

            things are probably best this way

```
things are probably best this way
```

     i said
I THINK IT WORKS BECAUSE OF THE NOISE

too busy with the sound
    of the sound
        to drown yourself

tiptoe on the edge
    of a steep cliff

~~I WILL TELL YOU WHEN I HAVE HAD ENOUGH~~

I WILL NOT BE SILENT

listen to the sound
    everything will tell you something

i am screaming
    because things are probably best this way

i am crying
    because none of this will last

i am laughing
    because suddenly everything is so bad it's good

nothing is what it seems

my ghost was nowhere to be found but the city lit the night bright illuminating the temples we built in each other's mouths where we worshipped &&& later pointed to spoons in the sky eating our fill with only our hands & hearts & i felt more animal than i had in years i felt more human than i had in years i felt more anything than i had in years this warm night full of breath & longing & old songs breathing new life new songs finding a way to the surface & the surface smooth & the songs the songs the songs we used to dance to sing-shouted from the fire escape & we push aside the thin layers of dust & ashes & rust where the pages of your past met the blank space of mine & we look for my ghost in the void of emptiness that we set out the next morning to fill with things that are better than bad in hopes she'd come back & we traveled the city hoping to see everything before discovering everything is in fact a very small thing we tried to pick up & hold in our hands despite the weight & the heft of trying to understand our own foundational cracks &&& in all the excitement i tripped & spilled blood &&& later you undressed the wounds & reminded me they need to breathe reminded me that air serves a purpose reminded me that stairs lead both up & down &&& after all that i woke up alone in a strange city with no money unsure what not to do next

```
my grief does not know how to sleep
```

*or even rest because it remembers
the tired faces of everyone we've loved
    as they turned in bed
    away from us
an army of beautiful sleepy angels
& how holy they glowed before
vanishing with the light*

*my grief does not know how to sleep
or even hold a flame but how it longs for a fire
    something we can hold against my body at night
instead of darkness
    something that meant
mourning was a time of day and not
the house we built together*

*my grief does not know how to sleep
because we are always preparing for an emergency
yet never quite ready for the worst and please
    don't tell my grief
but i swear i would replace it with a candle
if i could remember where i buried all the wax & wicks*

*my grief does not know how to sleep
and my least favorite part of the day is the hour
we say goodnight
    & return to our separate solitudes
the places we were born
where we become thoughtless & warm*

> *but this is also when i panic*
> *remembering i forgot to tell you one last time*

my grief does not know how to sleep
because it has turned my mind into an empty radio station
> *& it's static in my dreams & i know if we could sleep*
i would find myself wandering a deserted town
> *that ghosts won't even visit &*

unless you know where i am

i may never

wake up

so much can happen in a year

so we agree on one thing:

    that a year can last a long time

& days can freeze themselves to
    seasons in recurring patterns

i still wish you could have seen the tree
    that grew from the cracked floorboards
    of my bedroom all the way
    through the ceiling
        a staircase for sun and rain

if we were to ever agree on two things
    perhaps the second
    would be a belief in the inability to thwart fate

it is true i was cynical
    before lightning struck and
    the whole house caught fire

how i wish you could have seen
    the branches quivering

witnessed the arrival
    of a new kind of night

it could have been the first
    of many ways i would prove to you

        how good i am at ruining things

*an excuse to show you the exit to use
in case of emergency*

`missing: ghost`

my ghost has been missing for months. i put an ad in the paper that no one read. i call a mutual friend: have you seen my ghost? they don't know what i'm talking about. the house is very quiet. i do my best to distract myself. fold three thousand paper butterflies. i glue them to the wall and they fly away from me. the house is an exhibit. habitat for ghostless shell. every day i check the news for more bad news. i wonder when she'll come home. i am taking yet another depression bath. i think of her often. how she would have loved this. all the messes i'm making. i hallucinate the walls are caving in. i don't know what to do without her. i type WHAT IS REALITY *on a piece of paper until the words don't make sense. nothing is real and i know i know what I'm talking about. i know she would understand.*

can you hear me now

i still carry a typewriter from room to room as if it isn't now the year of zoom meetings & digital everything. we attempt to connect. screen to screen. your speakers aren't working so i type you a poem on scraps of paper & you read it to me line by line as the camera focuses. you are certain we are dreaming, which is both true and untrue. there isn't much we can do about anything. except stay home and cry a lot. EVERYTHING IS HAPPENING, *you read to me. i want to tell you everything. how bad it's been.* ~~this isn't about the pandemic. but no one knows that. not even you.~~ ARE WE DREAMING? *the post office is on fire. i can't stop thinking about all those letters, all those postcards that will never be read. no one comes to visit anymore.* WHAT NOW? *you ask me. my lips move but still no sound. i am saying: have you considered building a time machine? have you considered that time does not exist? have you considered that this is only one of a series of heartbreaking things to come? do you think we'll live through it? can you hear me now? once we counted jupiter's moons through a telescope lens. tried to imagine how small we are.* ~~every day i think about jumping.~~ I HAVE TO GO, *you read off the paper in my hand. it is true, i am afraid of what i am in/capable of. tonight i will dream i am a magnolia tree with dying branches. i will dream i am at the library and i am in love. i will dream we are dancing. i will dream of dark water and a storm. i will dream all this was a dream. we wave goodbye.*

we say goodbye to things

on sunday we rename the kitten
& leave the house to witness
    what brightness is left of the world
we [wander quiet woodland trails /
remember what it's like to breathe]
& make bouquets of dead flowers
    to surprise ourselves with later

my memory is weak & trembling
    every day holds [the key to an accident /
        the threat of slipping too far]
    every day i ask you what day it is

i say, tomorrow we will have a party
    (just us & the cats)
i think hard about baking a cake
i catch myself humming the tune
    of a song we used to dance to
        & uncle baby purrs

i justify my existence by sending letters
    by vowing [to create joy for humanity /
        to be kind to nature /
        to make things beautiful where i can /
        to tread lightly when i can't]
& i will do everything in my power to do better
    & i will write poems
        (whatever those are)

i make these promises knowing
nothing will ever be the same again

i know we are lucky
& it breaks my heart

WHAT NOW WHAT NOW WHAT NOW WHAT NOW WHAT NOW
WHAT NOW WHAT NOW WHAT NOW WHAT NOW WHAT NOW
WHAT NOW WHAT NOW WHAT NOW WHAT NOW WHAT NOW
WHAT NOW WHAT NOW WHAT NOW WHAT NOW WHAT NOW
WHAT NOW WHAT NOW WHAT NOW WHAT NOW WHAT NOW
WHAT NOW WHAT NOW WHAT NOW WHAT NOW WHAT NOW
WHAT NOW WHAT NOW WHAT NOW WHAT NOW WHAT NOW
WHAT NOW WHAT NOW WHAT NOW WHAT NOW WHAT NOW
WHAT NOW WHAT NOW WHAT NOW WHAT NOW WHAT NOW
WHAT NOW WHAT NOW WHAT NOW WHAT NOW WHAT NOW
WHAT NOW WHAT NOW WHAT NOW WHAT NOW WHAT NOW
WHAT NOW WHAT NOW WHAT NOW WHAT NOW WHAT NOW
WHAT NOW WHAT NOW WHAT NOW WHAT NOW WHAT NOW
WHAT NOW WHAT NOW WHAT NOW WHAT NOW WHAT NOW
WHAT NOW WHAT NOW WHAT NOW WHAT NOW WHAT NOW
WHAT NOW WHAT NOW WHAT NOW WHAT NOW WHAT NOW
WHAT NOW WHAT NOW WHAT NOW WHAT NOW WHAT NOW
WHAT NOW WHAT NOW WHAT NOW WHAT NOW WHAT NOW
WHAT NOW WHAT NOW WHAT NOW WHAT NOW WHAT NOW
WHAT NOW WHAT NOW WHAT NOW WHAT NOW WHAT NOW
WHAT NOW WHAT NOW WHAT NOW WHAT NOW WHAT NOW
WHAT NOW WHAT NOW WHAT NOW WHAT NOW WHAT NOW

a better world was possible

people are not a commodity. our joy is not for sale. living isn't easy. making friends is hard. our world is fractured. community care is rebellious. making art is a powerful tool for change. in our hearts. in our lives. in our world. making art for the people means it cannot be bought or sold. we must invite each other to live. there is more to life than what we've been told. they didn't want us to see a better world was possible. that chosen family can be a framework for revolution.

what if we crawled out from under these soiled boots, to blink at the sky, to hold each other. what if just being together could change everything. what if a better world was possible.

how we survived a pandemic

        never not a screen between us
        never not a masked [smile / frown]

what do we do?
what can we do?
they say the safest thing is to be safe
& it no longer feels right to be rebellious

when all this is over we'll throw a party
when all this is over we'll have a laugh
when all this is over we'll pretend we aren't traumatized forever

i haven't seen anyone in weeks besides the mailman bringing
    [holy notes /
    hateful bills /
    the neighborhood gossip]

the letters arrive slowly
but they arrive
HOW I MISS YOU
    i write

would this be an awkward time to tell you
    [in painstaking detail what you mean to me /
    what happened last winter /
    that i love you dearly /
    nothing at all]?

OH GODDAMN THESE TRYING TIMES

how worried should we be?

how worried should we be?
how worried should we be?

i've been casting more spells lately
hoarding ingredients
growing plants
learning how to [turn the earth /
* create fire /*
* breathe underwater]*

HOW VERY UNPRECEDENTED
what is to be done?

it could be worse, says everyone
it could be worse, says death closing in
it could be worse, we say as everything gets worse

it could be worse!
it could be worse!
it could be worse!

```
maybe my ghost is gone forever
```

we speak in postcard
       [WHAT A WORLD /
       HOW ARE YOU? /
       MORE SOON!]

i'm very lonely
whole months go by
& nothing happens
the news is relentless
my wheels spin
i go nowhere
i put on my mask
i go outside
       [we are all screaming /
       it is very quiet]

i'm no scientist

i don't even particularly want to live most days
but i'm invested in the story
       i want to know what happens
           how it all ends

& i want to burn by your side
       when the torches come
       when the end is nigh

special occasions

[too much / not enough] time has passed. it is another special occasion. we drive to the lake. nearly sunset when we arrive. we meet at the beach but stand at a distance. no touching. masks up. we wanted something to feel normal. so we're throwing a birthday party. under ominous clouds. everything that [has happened / is happening] is [still happening / still fresh]. i am distracted by the darkening water. i have been thinking about a letter i need to write. ~~i have been thinking about jumping~~. i can't hear what anyone is saying. nothing is normal. it begins to rain. i miss my ghost.

what we missed most

was the golden hour after the final bow. how we held each other. the lightness of the air. a turquoise bar full of beautiful ghosts howling. midnight clutching us. how we must have looked dancing. a hundred neon photographs. how we held each other. laughing. the joy in our faces. how we'd buy each other drinks with our last dollars and smile, raising our glasses. how the smoke rose to the rafters. how it almost killed us sometimes. how we kept at it. how we held each other. in the rumble of voices. our cups overflowing. the houselights dim. our glowing oasis. the ripple of movement. a frenzy of spirits. someone bursting into song. the flick of a match. how we held each other. how we could have gone home but we stayed. how we knew the spell would break. how we had to stay awake.

how we wanted it to last forever.

nothing will ever be the same

dearest: this is a difficult letter to write. the world is sick. i am sick. the wheels of sadness have been turning in my mind for quiet some time. despair. guilt. rage. existential dread. fear. isolation. repeat. i have gone mad trying to make sense of anything. in all the horror of this year, one thing sets it apart from all the horrors of all the other years: the distance between us. our sanctuary of togetherness, destroyed. i miss the comfort of your voice. rooms full of laughter. the medicine of a deep conversation / a good hug / nights dancing under the moon together, howling and alive. i miss feeling alive. i miss your stories / your songs / your fire. i miss going to your shows / your galleries / your kitchen. i miss the magic that can only happen when we are together. i wish i was not so affected by this loneliness, but i am. i am not myself. i worry about us, about you, every day. i started countless letters to you, but they were too sad, and i have never been good at asking for help. i want to tell you that every day, i try not to die. that some days it is all i can do. i want to tell you something that will make you smile, something that feels like a hug when you read it. i want to tell you that this will not be forever, because that is what i tell myself to get from one day to the next. tell me, what do you tell yourself? how are you getting by? how are you carrying your grief? how can i help? it is easy to be lost right now. so much is uncertain, so much out of our control. we can only do our best, which changes every day. for better or worse, nothing will ever be the same. i mourn what we had, our joy and our struggles. i will miss our time together the way one misses a secret: you could never know quite what it meant to me. i wish i could hold your hand and tell you the truth: that it was everything. a heavy burden and the brightest light, a rhythm, my heartbeat. i mourn the past so we may embrace the future. i mourn because i want us to survive.

```
self portrait as panic attack
```

the house is on fire & i can't find the cat & i'm late for an important meeting but i don't know what i'll say though i'm not sure i care because it's my birthday & i can cry if i want to & i had a party but no one came so i let the candles burn forever which is how we got here with the room on fire & instead of running from danger i'm remembering the sound of other people's voices & how i miss them unless of course we're in a crowded room with everything happening at once & nothing makes sense & then someone bumps me so hard i spill my drink & everyone stares in unbelievable silence as i burst into tears & use my clothes to clean the mess or what about that feeling of something brushing your ankle in a murky lake you fell into from a boat of questionable sturdiness & you shudder & scream for help just before being pulled under & now i can't breathe for the water & i can't breathe for the smoke as the fire swallows the landscape & turns my life's work to ash & a man is standing over me asking if i am okay but i don't know where i am or how the answers all came so easily before i was ever asked a question & how i was breathing fine until we were left alone & i saw the news today & i saw the news today & i saw the news today & i saw the news today & i saw the news today & i'm not sure what else i'm supposed to think about i'm not sure where this poem is going or why i write poems at all & i wonder if instead of writing poems i should be screaming then maybe everyone would know something is terribly wrong & do something what if we all screamed outside of the prisons & embassies & courthouses & banks & police stations what if we screamed inside of corporate offices & board rooms & internment camps & anywhere children are caged like animals & anywhere animals are bagged up like trash & what if we screamed at the whitehouse & in the bedrooms of the super rich & in the factories & warehouses that don't pay a living wage & in every government office what if we screamed until we collapsed do you think nothing would change do you think we'll ever be free

`self portrait as first poem on new medication`

everything still makes me cry

side effects include
  prophetic dreams
  dull sense of forgetting
    (is memory necessary?)
  increased awareness of bright colors & bedtime

planet: still burning
heart: still broken
humanity: still sick

  to not want to die is terrifying

nothing had changed and everything was different

*maybe she had been gone
long before she left*

*maybe my own silence
was the only thing left to blame*

suddenly the days were longer

*suddenly i was surrounded by birds
& wanted to learn their names*

*suddenly everything was [different / quiet]
& i guess i got used to it*

*i wish i could tell you
            [what still haunts me /
          that the danger has passed]*

*i wonder what do you call
the ghost of a ghost*

```
we did things we knew would kill us
```

that's just how it was. we could have everything our hearts desired delivered to our cozy houses & we never went outside. we [ate exotic fruit / burned oil / turned forests to landfills] like death was never an option. manufactured & tossed out mountains of trash. from cans to bins to trucks to [pits / oceans / prairies]. we [refused to share / made a lot of rules about nothing / were not afraid to invent god / were not afraid to play god] & had more food than we needed though most of us starved. we were so broken we didn't know we were alive. we were all connected but [pretended not to notice / didn't care]. we didn't [listen / love / learn) like we should have. we were miserable & acted surprised when everything seemed to go wrong even though we [had everything / were surrounded by everything / could do anything].

& yet we went on & on & on doing things we knew would kill us.

`missing: poet`

on my way to work today i fantasized again
    about taking a wrong turn and driving forever

i would go somewhere and reinvent my childhood

i would find my dead friends

my ghost was always itching to leave this place behind

both of us
    [hungry for excitement /
    longing for peace]

        (how i miss her most days)

i came here to write a book and ended up eating all the paper

a poem impossible inside this pulpy mass

i went looking for a pencil and never came back

do you remember
    [that we used to sing]?

do you remember
    [how we used to dance]?

do you remember
    [how drunk we were on living
    no matter how bad it got]?

```
laying awake at night thinking
about other people's lives
```

i have always been amazed
by how many other people there are

& i wonder

where they all go at the end of the day

& i wonder

does everyone else also expect the worst forever?

i am drowsy with hypervigilance

i try to file the memories of everything i've ever seen
       of everything that could ever happen
              without going under

i cry thinking about the faces of my friends

i miss people i haven't met

i hope everyone is sleeping well

EPILOGUE

`the end`

there are yet flowers
　　　though the world is burning
there is yet hope
　　　though we all will die

this life is a hallway of a thousand doors beckoning
　　　& we are the wandering
　　　　　may we find our way back

may the light that is in you
　　　meet the light that is in me
& make something beautiful
　　　& save something beautiful

listen to the earth
　　　who will tell you where it hurts

listen to the children
　　　who know best

listen
　　　though the world is burning & the crumbling has become your bones
listen
　　　even when everyone else has ceased to listen
listen
　　　though some things are lost forever
listen
　　　though birds are falling from the sky

there are yet flowers
    in simple places
        rising from concrete mistakes
there is still room for growth
    everywhere

        there is still hope

may the light that is in you
    meet the light that is in me
& make something beautiful
    & save something beautiful

there are yet flowers
    though the world is burning
there is yet hope
    though we all will die

acknowledgements

thank you, dear reader, for picking up this book. i know it is heavy but i hope you have found solace and connection in its pages: you are not alone. endless gratitude to em, sebastian, mike, and tim for reading the earliest drafts & for being thoughtful and gentle with them. thank you cameron and aaron for making it beautiful. thank you connie for your supportive heart and for letting me read to you. thank you community for your love. thank you pandemic pen pals, thank you comrades against injustice, thank you witches & poets & artists for inspiring hope in my weary heart. i love you all. && of course thank you forever to darin and the goliad team for believing in me & this book & making all of this possible. there are yet flowers.

courtney marie is a writer & artist based in denton, texas. they are the author of don't get your hopes up (2018, Thoughtcrime Press) and songs we used to dance to (2022, Goliad Media). their work has appeared in Nat Brut, The Boiler, Thimble Literary Magazine, and beyond. cm enjoys making weird & sentimental art with/for their community, exploring the world, and playing pinball. they live with three cats, cry all the time, and are forever writing letters & sending snail mail in a desperate attempt to connect with the outside world. they are the co-founder & director of the artist collective spiderweb salon.

www.ingramcontent.com/pod-product-compliance
Lightning Source LLC
Chambersburg PA
CBHW070432010526
44118CB00014B/2004